# LIFE IN THE RETIREMENT BED
## OF
## ROSES

### Georgia B. Watson

Rainbow Books/Betty Wright
Moore Haven, Florida
1982

Illustrator: Jeff Black
Cover Design: Lu Hollander
Produced by M. Lyn Ratzlaff
Copyright 1982 by Georgia B. Watson
Published by RAINBOW BOOKS/Betty Wright
2299 Riverside Drive
P.O. Box 1069
Moore Haven, Florida 33471-1069

Printed in the United States of America.
All rights reserved. No part of the
publication may be reproduced, stored in a
retrieval system, or transmitted, in any
form or by any means, electronic, mechanical,
photocopying, recording, or otherwise, without
the prior written permission of the publishers.

Library of Congress:
Catalog Card No. 81-84831
ISBN: 0-935834-06-0

## DEDICATION

*Dedicated to 35,000 students from whom I learned so much and from whom I retired early. Worn to a nub after 40 years of it. Thanks anyway.*

*And to my colleagues P.C., D.W. and P.C., the kingmakers, incognito.*

# CONTENTS

SEX ................................................ 11

JUST SMOKE ........................................ 15

AROUND HOME ................................... 25

KEEPING UP WITH THINGS ...................... 37

POT ART .......................................... 47

AWAY FROM HOME .............................. 61

REAPING THE HARVEST ......................... 79

SAVE FACE ........................................ 87

NO DOUBT ABOUT IT ............................ 97

# LIFE IN THE RETIREMENT BED OF ROSES

# SEX

## SEX

I've been advised to put a bit of sex in this book if I want it to sell. If I do, it will have to be about rats. The voice of experience is the only one to be raised on such a topic. I do know, from experience, if female rats get too hot, they eat their babies. If male rats get too cold, there are no babies. In a laboratory experimenting with rats, happiness goes up and down with the temperature.

Make of it what you will. That's my pitch. Any little hints you find in this book to help you avoid the thorns as you toss around in the retirement bed of roses, feel free. Help from any source should be cherished, but watch that thermometer!

# SEX

I've been advised to put a bit of sex in this book. If I want to sell, I do it, it will have to be about rats. The sum of experience is the only one to be touched on such a topic. I do know from experience, if female rats get too hot, they eat their babies. If male rats get too cold, there are no babies. In a laboratory experiment, suffer a happiness, go up and down with the temperature.

Make of what you will. That's my point. Another little hints you find in this book to help you avoid the thorns as you toss around in the euphoriant bed of roses. Feel free. Help from any source should be cherished, but watch that thermometer.

# JUST SMOKE

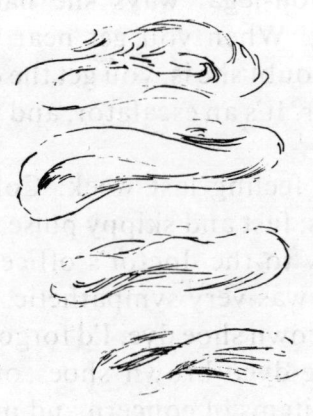

## JUST SMOKE

    No place provides a better opportunity to bump into retired friends than the grocery store. This morning a cart insisted on coming in my direction. It was driven by an acquaintance just out of the hospital minus her gall bladder. She had her diet needs in large print on white cards. After our carts bumped, and we had given each other a Russian kiss salute, she detailed to me why her glasses are no good now. During her recent surgery the wrong nerve got deadened and has never awakened. As a result she can only read large black print. In addition to selecting baby food for her supper she seemed to be drumming up moral support for a malpractice suit against the surgeon. Having a pretty good idea about the location of my gall bladder and being certain the optic nerve isn't even close, I had to rupture her legal plans or abandon my buggy and exit. I exited. She is the type conversationalist who keeps saying, "Don't you agree?" and won't accept "Hum" as an answer.

In some non-legal ways she had my sympathetic understanding. When you get near the top of the age ladder, as no doubt she is, you get the distinct impression it's not a ladder. It's an escalator, and you are about to be dumped.

I had that feeling last week. Cold hands and feet, brown toenails, fast and skippy pulse, and blurred vision sent me slowly to the doctor's office for a demise date prognosis. He was very sympathetic. He even looked at my toenails. Brown shoe dye. I'd forgotten about wearing my once white-dyed-brown shoes out in the rain. He checked other items of concern and predicted no funeral soon. He did say unless I stopped driving like a terrapin somebody was going to knock me into Heaven. It seems he had been driving behind me on the way to his office.

However, he called the hospital lab and told them to expect me early next morning, sans breakfast, to have a blood inspection. I went. The technicians withstood my expressions of agony and swooning off. They stuck me every hour on the hour. My blood looked okay to me, and I was about to go AWOL, after the ten o'clock tapping when the fire alarm sounded. We were informed via the loud speaker the fire was in the lab. All personnel trained to fight fire were to go at once to the lab with fire extinguishers and lock the doors, while they searched for the fire. Being locked in, there was no way to avoid the eleven o'clock blood letting and filling the little white cup in the rest room. The rest room door had no lock. Fireproof clad figures kept interrupting, looking for something to extinguish.

I finally dragged my bloodless body out of the hospital at noon as the all clear sounded. Some dope had dropped a cigarette butt in the elevator hole. No fire. Just smoke. My healthy concerns were also just smoke — created by sitting around the house counting my pulse while I examined my toenails.

Having my veins punched isn't an event ever anticipated with pleasure. So far as I can detect there has been no reduction in needle size nor technique improvement over the years. They still suck the blood out with a long needle on a hit and miss basis. The odds are fifty-fifty the first aim will be a miss. It would hurt less if they just made a cut and let me drip into something.

But after a trip to the dentist I feel better and smile bigger with clean teeth, clean caps, shiny crowns and bright clasps. These things are worth preserving, but the real satisfaction comes from the capital gain contained therein. My oral cavity is filled with $30 an ounce gold. That $1500 capital gain may be safer there than keeping it in a sock under the mattress.

Not everyone feels so good about dental investments. One acquaintance informed me she had gone flat-headed from pushing on the whiplash pillow. No longer does she have a nicely shaped, round head. She says when he starts at her mouth with a concealed weapon in his hand, she presses. Not only does this make her flat-headed but side-wider, and her ears stick out. There was very little I could say of a comforting nature. I had never known her when her head was round, and her ears closely hung. I could see a bit of change from the front view. Her upper lip seems to give toward the right side. This is hardly noticeable because of a cauliflower development underway in the lower lip.

I told her a bit of head and mouth distortion was a small price to pay for creative dental work. She could have the shanks of her glasses changed to fit the moving ears.

Now that my mouth is okay, I can worry about my feet. My podiatrist has me in walking wedgies with thick rubber bottoms, and that's not the kind of a sole I want to turn toward the congregation at the communion rail on Sunday. But he says if I come for the next whirl and trim with new corns and recurled toes, he is going to give up on my feet. I don't want that to happen. He has good, healing ways. Especially do I like that final foot rub with green stuff. The answer seems to be for me to overcome ego, get my name on the infirm list and be seat-served on communion Sunday.

Skin blemishes are also little thorns among my retirement roses. A small item in a magazine urging attention to sleeping volcano malignancies of the skin sent me to a dermatologist to have a neck doodad cut off and assayed. The lab report gave an all clear, but the removed thing had roots. The crater must be covered with a collar or scarf. More removals, and I could end up looking like a female Moslem in rubber sole wedgies being pew-served communion. I'm hesitating on the face clean up.

I'd like to attain a riper old age but want to keep my concerns about my health healthy. Not eating the red cherry in a glass of something is perhaps taking it too far. Now something real, like the news that a caffeine drinking female may place unborn babies in danger, alerts me. It doesn't take long to go from dangers of caffeine to the six or eight weeks old fetus to wondering what it has done to a non-fetus out in the world drinking everything listed as having caffeine in it. That would be 3,380 weeks of contamination. There was not enough evidence in the article to give clues as to what should be checked for damage from caffeination. Some of the inadequacies attributed to age just may be caffeine implemented. Makes me wonder. If I stop drinking coffee, etc. and become decaffeinated, will the effects be reversed? Unanswered questions like that can throw mental health into a decline if repined on.

At the moment my mental health seems to be on a par with the general population. I worry a bit now and then, but finally arrive at the end of the tunnel by telling myself, "If you couldn't do it thirty years ago why agitate now?" Inadequacies of long standing are still standing. Like stretching dollars from the first to the first. I get a big mental decline in the middle of the month. Sound advice about saving and stretching must come from experts who don't have my deeply rooted impulses which make me expensive to operate.

I regret the exit of the small grocery store. Phoning an order read from a list and having the things delivered to the door made it easier on the shopper who couldn't resist three for a dollar bargains. I'm not good at listening when my mental unit flashes an alert warning me to spend only the 35 cents for one can of peas.

Occasionally I lie awake for a few minutes thinking about not having any grandchildren. This happens after being shown lots of cute kids in photo albums at some grandmother's house. Since I don't have any children, I just say to myself, "You want a miracle?" and go to sleep. Sometimes I can point out to myself how much the pictures I saw favor the grandmother. Not having any then turns into a blessing to count. Beats counting sheep.

Some of my friends hang on to mental well-being by having pets. I like that. I can enjoy feeling cold noses, talking back to parrots, chucking cats under the chin, and go home. I had a dog once. He was half Pekingese and half otherwise. His legs were so short he dragged —unless the leash was a belly band. Taking him for a walk meant lifting the middle all the way. He got too heavy to be walked, and I gave him away.

There are many ways to maintain good, healthy mental perspective. Exercise until you're too tired to think is one avenue. If you are short-winded, this won't do. Some people bite fingernails, some smoke, some drink, some fiddle with things and so on. I have one friend who saves pennies. She says when she is blue-deviled, she rolls pennies to take to the bank. She can't think about anything while so engaged or she spatters pennies everywhere.

"Do something" seems to be the rule for all of us. After dashing through doing nothing, I find a taste of it constitutes enough. Do nothing may lead to lifting the voice of wisdom and moralizing about the good old days. When that happens, get busy. Being bored with self can best be handled by tackling physical things beyond your level of expertise. Like skiing. It is very difficult to keep the balance between a healthy mind and a healthy body on the ski slopes. Prudence is of the essence on this tight rope of age. Sometimes it may be better to just sit down and scream. Especially if the choice involves a broken ankle as feet go in opposite directions. Mental health gets in the same bed with physical health — when things like that happen.

How am I to know when I'm healthy? Apparently only unhealthy conditions can be determined. Who goes to a medical doctor and/or a head shrinker to find out how healthy he is? I go to find out how sick I am, and what may be the expectations for recovery. It's that word *recovery*. If I've had a fever and it goes away, I'm healthy? Even if my lower limbs feel like spaghetti? If I've been seeing pink elephants and they vanish, am I now mentally okay? How about beginning to think some of my friends look like haddocks? Or this feeling I'm slipping through time without living up to the Girl Scout Creed learned at the age twelve?

Another little problem of the thinking kind may continue to bug you. What happened to those retirement leisure hours you dreamed about when you were a paycheck employee? The things you now do may have no identity with the "when-I-retire" dream. Sampling the lifestyle of the non-working population can get you into quicksand. Even if you don't enjoy whatever it is you are doing you just keep on. Especially if it happens to be something not beyond your level of performance. The whole world of activity is spread out like a cafeteria food display. The chicken salad is good, so close in on it and eat chicken salad every day. In looking back over the last few weeks I see I've slipped into a bunch of doings that run counter to the things I really enjoy. The phone rings and someone has a great plan for tomorrow, for their own entertainment. When it is the last thing among all things that I want to do, why do I say okay? Maybe we need to firm up and start a few plans for use of our own retirement hours. Like just sitting.

I guess there are two extremes of using this free time we worked so long to buy. One is doing nothing, because there isn't anything we want to do. I call this unmotivated nothing, a big part of my "when-I-retire" dream. This breaks the closing-in circle of plans for my doing nothing thought up by someone else and lets me think up things on my own that I'd rather put nothing in place of.

No doubt about it, the shadow of health gets longer and blacker as birthdays come and go. I've just decided to be healthy when I'm worried about things and people other than myself. Even if they look like haddocks.

# AROUND HOME

AROUND HOME

## AROUND HOME

One thing you can do, if you sit around the house worrying about things, is nibble yourself to death. Food consumption between meals gradually increases. Try working out a balanced daily diet composed of peanuts, cheese crackers, marshmallows, chocolate pinwheels, potato chips, party mints, pralines and toasted pecans. If you can't analyze these delights into a balance — then change to rabbit nibbles one half-day. Carrot and celery strips. It didn't work for me. I had to force my reaching. When I put something like potato chips between the carrots and celery, I never got back to the celery. Just ate all the chips. You may have better luck.

It isn't just that the nibbling is detrimental to health, which of course it is because it keeps one from eating the proper foods at the proper time, but the budget suffers too. Trying to stretch dollars and shrink fat should go hand-in-hand and be quite compatible. Don't give up.

I've thought one answer to this dilemma might be to

spend more time working outside and less time wearing out the chair springs, watching to-be-continued real life drama.

Be careful with the selection of outside involvement. Start easy. Cleaning gutters should be undertaken after you have exercised your knees to the point of being able to get down after you get up. One of my retired colleagues over-extended himself. The sun blistered his head and nose before his wife returned from a party and helped his feet locate the ladder steps.

Some of the troublesome things I'm running or walking into have arisen because of the freedom to work around home in daylight. Probably you, too, have never seen your living quarters except on Saturday and Sunday, and those were not outside work days. Cleaning gutters and chores like that received attention only when a neighbor informed me she was having a yard cleaning and did I want to be next on the yard man's list. That system worked fine. And would work again if I stopped telling myself, "You can do that and save thirty dollars." But, believe me, one by one, those little jobs tackled with retirement gusto have regained a position on the "have-it-done" list. Cleaning gutters is on my list just below mowing the grass.

Mowing is now a pay somebody job because it became too expensive for self-operation. First expenditure was a gasoline lawn mower with a string starter. If it ever started, it was easy to push. But it only started once. Wrong mixture or something. It was traded for an electric with a 100-foot cord. The lot is 200 feet deep with the house in the middle and thirty-two trees scattered. After the third cord cutting, an ad was placed in the paper listing a practically new electric lawn mower for sale. The advice here is have it done. It costs less.

Another little hint may save some embarrassment. Be

very careful about the arm movement you use to throw out the lawn fertilizer. You may come up with a design in the grass that will stop the traffic. I used an across the chest motion and now have a yellow and green striped lawn. People don't stop. They just slow down.

Don't have your get-out-doors energy spurt too late in the spring. Such things as trimming the shrubbery should be done before new growth appears. Foresight is better than hindsight, when the result is irreversible.

If you need to use bricks to line flower beds or to stop a soil wash, buy bricks with no holes. I'm familiar with a holes-in brick border emplaced as a retainer. When it rains the effect is one of shower heads lining the flower bed on the outside. All the top soil is oozing through the holes into the yard next door.

Bricklaying may make you decide you aren't the outdoor yard work type. The physical result can be the inability to go either up or down from the deep squat position, and you will want to try your luck with indoor bloomers when your raw fingers heal.

Other people plant little bulbs in pots, set them in a dark closet, remove them about ten days before Christmas and bingo. On schedule those bulbs turn into beautiful whatever they are supposed to be, looking just like the picture in the catalogue from which they were ordered. I gave it a try, following the instructions to the letter. One bulb went into the closet after having been planted with loving care. She died there. Some of my interior growing efforts were fruitless because I forgot to water them. But that dead bulb is a mystery to me. Nothing was done to kill it. I just left it be.

Ferns in clay pots that have to be toted back and forth from indoors to outdoors as the temperature goes up and down seem to be very hard to kill. But even they know when a green thumber has them in hand. Such a blessed neighbor looked after our two ferns for a few weeks last summer. They grew so much she had to put them in larger pots. She said they had been pot-bound for some time. Until I saw the results of her care, I thought they looked pretty good. If you have ferns you should buy larger pots to have on hand in case your thumb is green.

To become more knowledgeable about how to grow all kinds of things watch Crockett's Victory Garden on PBS television. Last week I enjoyed watching Mr. Crockett start seedling beds indoors. His indoors must be a greenhouse. He has beds that are identified, and he has little tools at hand. He covers seed with a little soil, then straw, and when on later programs he digs through the straw, there is always something sprouting exactly where he spades in. Living rooms usually aren't large enough for this type planting, but you can try that seed bit in an outdoor spot. I planted squash seed and covered the bed with pine needles. I never found a thing when I dug. I don't like squash anyway. Just in case the squash sprouts were inhibited by an unloving thumb it might be wise for you to plant something you can look forward to eating with pleasure.

Interest in plants and gardening comes on strong every spring. In addition to watching Crockett I go right to the handbook for gardeners to learn the difference between an annual and a perennial. Don't wait too late. By January things you want to plant should be in their permanent growing beds. Especially pansies. If it is March, you are too late. They are annuals, and that means, if you want any, you have to plant them once a year. Perhaps a switch to perennials would be helpful. Like daisies. They just keep coming up. But the book warns some of them won't. You plant the seed for flowers the next year. And that is it. Then you start over.

As a retiree, you'll be expected to putter around the

house, inside and out. It is deemed healthy to be concerned about growing things and keeping all visible areas in shipshape.

But there are other things to add to the list of around the house retirement concerns. Your brain should get the message you have retired and are in the market for a new sleep pattern. The 10:00 p.m. go-to-bed signals seem to want to keep on coming, and if not answered, you'll fall out of your chair. That isn't as annoying as the 6:00 a.m. signal to get up and hop-to-it. To be in a motivational alert at that time of day is terrible. Here are a few suggestions in answer to the hop-to-what dilemma: clean out dresser drawers; try to balance your checkbook; run the sweeper under the dining room table; squeeze those oranges before they rot; polish silver; try to read the cookbooks friends gave you for Christmas; go through the Goodwill bag once more to see if you are giving away anything you just might could use; find the big magnifying glass and check the word *Liberty* on your Indian Head cents to see if you have any VF's; call retired friends and say wrong number.

I tried that last one with a little difference. My notion was to make a survey to see what the reaction would be to organizing an "Early Bird Club." The effort was non-productive. Friends who answered the 5:30 a.m. phone call made some suggestions: "Go to bed at 4:00 a.m.;" "Seek employment in an all-night business not requiring much expertise;" "Go jump in a lake;" "Soak your head;" "Bake a cake;" "Plan a trip." Buy a yo-yo seemed to be the best suggestion submitted by ex-friends. They were not interested in a club. I bought a yo-yo.

Modern yo-yo strings get worse tangles than those of some decades ago. After working an hour and a half with the thing this morning at six, I went back to bed exhausted and slept into a 10:30 disaster. Pampered, sluggish bathroom drains had arrived at full stop. The plumber was called. He arrived with his committee of helpers, explored under the house, rendered a verdict, "Tree roots," and left. Curious about what had taken place, I crawled under to take a look. Fortunately light came through the air grills and there was no collision with one of the committee members who was still under there. I turned on my side to face his side, and the conversation went like this.

"Hello. Didn't know you were under here. What's going on?"

"I'm holding the plug in the drain valve hole."

"Why? Won't the plug stay in?"

"No, ma'am. We had trouble getting it out and stripped the threads."

"How long do you have to hold it?"

"My partners have gone to see if they can find a new one. I don't think they can. When was the house built?"

"1956," I said. "What happens if they can't find one? You can't just live under here with your hand in that hole." I had visions of having to crawl under and feed him three times a day.

"We'll plug it with cement."

Not being able to think of anything else to say, I backed out. The search committee returned with no plug and permanently sealed the drain hole with cement. Everyone departed. I counted them. Now uneasy thoughts about the cement in that rooter hole worry me everytime I use the bathroom. I would like to get the roots out of that sewer for peace of mind, even if it's draining.

If you live in a house planned by you, built under your loving eye without benefit of an architect, it is full of your own mistakes. Some of them are original, some are the accidents of expediency and some are acts of God. For example, for expediency the driveway, four inches of concrete, covers the main sewer line for a few feet. The gas, water and sewer lines, originally coming in from the street through flat unplanted-to-be-lawn, are now covered by four twenty-five year old dogwood trees and two big oaks. Only God can make a tree, but it takes a landscaper to plant them exactly over all the pipes. I wanted a new sewer line from the house to the street. It can be done, yes. All we have to do is cut four dogwood trees, two big oaks and remove the stumps and all the roots. The decision was made to leave man's pipes, sewers and God's trees alone, and call for the rotor-rooter as needed. There must be some way to get the cement out of that valve hole under the house.

Mice may add to your at home problems. Nobody has made a better mouse trap. The little old traps are so messy and so expensive. My budget includes one dozen mouse traps. Used mouse traps are non-existent where I reside, because no one will remove the mouse. The trap and contents are wrapped in newspaper and discarded. My solution to the problem calls for someone to develop a beam that would disintegrate the mouse into a small bit of ash, and leave the trap and cheese intact. I've added cheese to the plan, because cheese costs more than the trap. The beam would save on Bandaids, too. I've never set a trap without premature activation on my finger at least once.

It would be better to halt the trek of the mice from outdoors to indoors when cold weather hits. This plan would substitute a cat for the indoor trap. The big problem with this idea is modern cats don't know a mouse from a hole in the ground. The cat with which I'm best acquainted lives up the street but sleeps on the hood of my car. Firewood is stacked under the carport. Under the wood is where the mice gather before seeking an entrance into the house. I watched that cat open one eye, turn over and go back to sleep when a log was pulled off the top of the pile and disturbed the mouse colony. Three of them ran out in plain view, paused, and then took off for the bushes. Neither the cat nor I knew what to do.

It's a small thing, but in the right hands an improved killing device for the little pests could give us leverage in such things as oil from OPEC. "You cut your prices—we'll likewise your mices."

You'll find yourself going from one crisis to another as you sit around home. In the good old days of having to go to work, the service people were called, came, and corrected, and all you had to do was pay the bill, when it came in. Now you watch them work, and you fret.

This month has been constantly fretting because of having a new roof put on. No problems with the roof, but those little pipes on top of the house can give you fits. Some of them have little four-cornered hats. They are the gas fumes exhaust route. Those without the hats exhaust from places like bathrooms and the kitchen sink, and they don't bother. But those gas fumes roof appendages must go back down into the similar attachment on, for example, the water heater. Just giving them a push from the top won't do. I've sniffed for three days trying to find the source of a very peculiar odor. I found it. Ill-connected gas venter because the inside pipe was bent. Result: new water heater.

Then the vacuum cleaner developed a fifth wheel, right in the center. When I finished pushing it around in one room, I was exhausted and the rug results were not good. Just a five-on-the-floor pattern with string, etc. that I was trying to get up, still in the tracks. Taking the sweeper to the repair man resulted in a slipped discus diagnosis. The slipped part was dragging in the middle. It could be fixed, but it would cost almost as much as a new machine. Right. We now have a new vacuum cleaner.

You might be wise to use an old fashioned broom and dispose of floor cleanings under the rug. The trouble is whatever you have had for 30 years is what you're stuck with until it poops. I've decided to keep inside cleaning at a very low activity level. Once you get in it too deep, it's just like opening a can of worms or finding one little moth in the closet. You empty all closets and spray, when all you needed to do was kill one moth. In case there are others — kill on appearance.

Chain reactions from housework are the things we must look out for. Don't start anything that leads to something else. You clean out one drawer or wash one window, and where are you?

The same wisdom should be applied in the yard. Just trim the shrub and leave it alone. You could spray and fertilize and water and clip the grass. If you do that for all things, inside and out, you'll be ready for a tent on a little piece of pavement.

There are nice things about being at home. You get to know people who live close by. Having friendly neighbors is great, but getting rid of produce you don't want presents somewhat of a problem. Last week an across-the-street neighbor came over with a gift of one eggplant. Thanks were duly given for the beauty. Not knowing what to do with it, I took it next door and left it at the rear entrance with a "hope you can use this" note. In one hour that eggplant visited four places and was back with the neighbor who started it. When she called to relate the eggplant journey, I suggested she invite us all over for supper and serve it.

# KEEPING UP WITH THINGS

## KEEPING UP WITH THINGS

During the World Series this year, I had time to pay attention to runs batted in records. The most valuable player award went to the man who got his fellow teammates home safe. I thought it was very kind of the statisticians to make it possible to finger the right fellow for that honor. As a baseball fan I'm usually more interested in scores than runs batted in figures.

I couldn't help but compare this baseball record with my own in the matrimony game. I don't know how many runs I've batted in, but I'm in the zero scoring column. Once I was fifty feet from the altar as a flower girl in a wedding in 1916.

I've never taken a vow to endow anybody with my worldly goods until death do us part. The only promises of that nature I've made have been to mortgage companies with stipulations providing insurance for payment in case of my demise. So far, none of my mortgage vows has led to payments of that kind. I'm still tied, but if I wanted to, I could sell my vow papers. I am told by friends who have several times heard those beautiful words — you may kiss the bride — there is no out except through legal channels when the love, honor and pay vows begin to pall. Too bad the partners who signed the paper can't just sell off each other. The wife could keep whatever she got for the husband, at an auction, and vice versa. This would be non-discriminatory. Anybody could submit a bid. Couples without issue probably would get uncoupled faster.

Naturally I'm without issue, being a spinster. I also am short on close relatives. Most of them are interred. My problem is finding a place to leave my equities. These will become 100 percent ownership, courtesy of the insurance companies, when I die. In addressing the problem, I've found several institutions of higher learning who will, for X number of promised assets, eulogize and name a chair for me before I go. After I go, my ghost can share the seat with a live professor. Or I can turn my equities into cash and fan embers now —if I think there is a spark there.

My Last Will and Testament reflects this confusion. You would think anybody could make a Will. I can, I did and I still do. I am never sure the current edition is the final copy. I read everything printed about the pitfalls in this endeavor. To date, every Will I've made has been in a pit. I've asked my attorney to omit the word "Last" on my new Will.

I'm about to make another addition. It addresses the problem of disposal of remains. My choices have increased from two to three. I was prepared to choose between ground and scattering with ground about to win, because of ancestor influence. They are all placed head east, feet west, in ordinary cemetery plots, with tombstones giving data about the departed one who lies thereunder. The crematorium route had not received much consideration until I read an article saying scattering the ashes is first in terms of least costly of the three. Interring in the ground is second cheapest with mummification, the third choice, the most costly. It seems they now can prepare the remains, using an old Egyptian formula, and place the resulting mummy, me, in a see-through glass case. I've eliminated becoming a mummy, dead or alive. And I just may include both of the other two. The provision would read, "If it is raining, burn and scatter. If the sun is shining, bury me in the ground."

Last Will and Testament problems can be confounded by inability to keep up with assets. Especially current worth in liquidity terms. This situation arises when we have a tad of money lovingly thought of as savings. We can enjoy thinking about it after going to bed. Like the cow chewing her cud. But no more. Accumulated liquidity chases higher interest in so many places I forget where it is today. The fun of having money is to be able to count it and figure the interest. I've figured interest on my $1000 funeral fund at everything on a percent scale from 5 to 18 with compounding daily, weekly, monthly and not. If interest rates continue to bounce, I'm going to bring my money home, count it, and let it help equities fan embers. And to heck with what it costs to inter my remains!

Another bit of irksome record keeping has to do with having the car washed. I drive out a nervous wreck after watching that big brush come at me, but manage to open the glove compartment and safely store the ticket. One dollar off on the next wash if used before a certain date. I've never made it.

Even making my checkbook agree with the money keepers at the bank has me in a flutter. I signed up for that NOW or some such initials, meaning they pay interest on the checking account. I forget to add it to my balance and work my little calculator to shreds going backwards into infinity to find a $12.13 error.

Then, too, there is that matter of bills to be paid. Instead of coming in on the first of the month as expected, they now scatter all over the calendar. I never know when I'm through or whether I have enough left to eat out once. It may be more convenient for the billers, but it cuts into payer pleasure.

Stamps have just been added to my list of confusions. I still have a few twelve, thirteen, fourteen and fifteen cent stamps. Just try making twenty cents out of that. Or even figuring out what to buy to get each category out of the kitchen drawer and onto a letter, whatever the current rate may be. I'm never sure. Recently I saved postage by sending postal cards to a dozen friends inviting them to drop by for conversation and refreshments. Each of them had to pay two cents to get to read the card. The fact they had to pay postage made a good conversation topic as they dipped into the dip with chips. General agreement was reached. They ate their two cents worth. "Send invitations short on postage anytime," was the departure comment. As hostess I took that as a very good indication the guests had enjoyed the party.

Also in that kitchen drawer of confusing things are the numbers I've been assigned that make me eligible to win a trip to Alaska or someplace with a million dollars to spend while there. Some of them are five years old, and I've renewed several times whatever it is they want me to receive. Hope springs eternal, but I do wonder occasionally how patient one should be. How long should you keep those sweepstake numbers?

The blank on the income tax form where they ask for occupation is causing a problem. Last year I wrote retired. I didn't especially care for that so this year I wrote unoccupied. I'm not happy with that, and I'm sure they won't be. It sounds so political, like non-aligned. Next year, if all retirees write unemployed in the blank, it will throw the national figures off, but it sounds better than retired which smacks of withdrawing or being phased out.

Probably the retiree should ask, "Why do you want to know?" If the point is to see whether we are collecting money for services rendered, why don't they ask us? Then we could say no. Since the small box to indicate a specific age has been checked they should be able to add two and two. It would be very unlikely income is being stored under the mattress or someplace, even if the blind box were left unchecked.

I could simplify the tax form for them. Every year they tell us how much easier it will be to meet that April deadline alive, and it never is. So why not: How much did you earn? *0*. How much do you owe us? *0*. Then there would be no worrying about occupation by me or them. I do nothing and earn likewise.

At one time in my salary days I wondered who "they" were. I found out. "They" lived in an office someplace and used a computer to spit me out. Then there was a death message which was difficult to open, because I developed the shakes. They wanted a little chat with me about a claimed dependent they thought was a watchdog. I was to take my records to the Federal Building, room 408, to be examined. The checker was a middle-aged male with a liver disorder or a cheating wife. Upon leaving I had visions of being attired in slacks with a stripe up each side leg cutting grass along one of the county roads or maybe on the interstate road gang. I still have those visions. It's been eight years, and I've received no verdict.

My advice, which I now follow, don't put anything on that tax form to upset the computer. Auditors earn a living checking these spit-outs. Just one little old thing, like a dependent poodle, seems to stimulate their "search and find" dander.

When that once a year income tax business is added to other paper work usually related to it, you get a pile of paper. I've attempted to evolve a filing system to assist in eliminating the confusion. To date, my success is minimal, but you may want to try it. The only file from which I've been able to find anything is the sharp pointed one called a stick. That is okay except seven sticks take up a lot of room on a small desk. It takes five for income tax records, one for things not to forget to do and one for miscellaneous, not fitting any place else. My tax sticks are labeled: (1) medical and anything remotely related thereto; (2) receipts for contributions which can no longer be avoided by saying, "I gave at the office;" (3) professional activities such as having the typewriter greased; (4) slips from Goodwill, the Library, etc., recording the value of unloaded items; (5) bank notes, taxes, mortgage interest and things like that. I include the slips showing the amount of sales tax paid. This is in anticipation of being able to deduct more than the measly bit they specify in those little tables.

If you use the stick file system you must be orderly about searching the file for a receipt or something which is usually first on. The big problem is getting the paper reestablished with the stick coming out the old hole. Last year I discovered four holes in my bank note. One of them went exactly through the amount of interest paid the bank. That bothers the IRS and in turn the bank when asked for a copy of the note.

Another record keeping chore involves those "use before *(date)*" products. The only thing they seem to have overlooked and omitted requiring a death date on is toothpaste. Last night I used nose drops that had been dead two years. No harm, no good, so what's the difference? Why make us put on glasses or get a magnifying glass and scrutinize every little bottle in the medicine cabinet? If dates must be checked before using, they should include information about what to do with the expired stuff. If flushed away, it might eat the pipes. If thrown in the garbage, it could kill a pig.

I made a discovery in investigating dates on things in the medicinal line. A well-known laxative firm short-changed the buyer on the expiration date by about sixteen months. The activity ingredients were not depleted.

Food date recording can be done on a sheet of paper taped to the door of the refrigerator. Examination this morning revealed the coffee cream is to be discarded on the 27th of this month. So are the eggs. That gives me two days to use a pint of cream and eat sixteen eggs.

Sometimes I have a spell of to-heck-with-it and give up on the food dates. When that happens, I revert to non-consumer protection methods of smell, taste and look. This is almost foolproof anyway. If the yellow part of the egg breaks and I haven't stuck my thumb in it, I throw it out regardless of the date the hen finished her work.

# POT ART

POP ART

## POT ART

In between thinking up things to do to the Internal Revenue Service, worrying about wills and trying to remember where savings are currently deposited, I'm busy developing a grocery list to fit the $10 left in the food kitty. This is a new activity for me. At a somewhat younger age a dash by the grocery store on the way home from work produced a T-bone, salad stuff, French bread, a baking potato and sour cream for supper. Upon request the meat person happily cut a good thick steak. Now when he sees me coming he disappears into that back room where they keep the dead cow hanging. Punching the button that says, "RING FOR SERVICE", takes a lot of courage. The last time I handed him a pork chop to cut in half, lengthwise, he looked like he was going to throw his cleaver at me. Current financial circumstances lead me to pass up expensive delicacies, including chicken wings. There are at least four different good ways to cook wings: barbecue, fry, bake or boil and make chicken stew.

They now cost so much, I only give them a quick look on the way to the ground beef.

The vegetable people don't seem to be any happier with my shopping list pattern. They will weigh a fourth of a pound of green beans, and they will open a ten-pound sack of potatoes and let me pick one, but they give the impression it's hard for them to keep "the customer is always right" philosophy.

In salary days cooking was never my long suit. My culinary efforts were few and far between. The kitchen was the place to plug in the coffee pot, squeeze juice, drop bread in a toaster, eat, rinse the dishes and run. Last week in a move to change a kitchen life style, I baked a pound cake. When that cake came from the oven, I had my first feeling of pride that comes with being a domesticated female who has just produced. I looked at that beautiful cake and had visions of flooding the neighborhood with cake slices and a sprig of greenery carrying a label "From the Kitchen Of" and my name. The middle sank four inches and the cake died as I stood there watching. Eight ounces of that pound disappeared.

I gave that cake my best effort. George Spencer's statement in his *LATIN LESSONS*, published in 1845 by *Pratt, Woodford & Co.*, N.Y. expresses my feelings exactly.

"Either I will conquer thee or be conquered by thee."

The cake conquered. (This quotation is used without permission. A letter to the publisher was returned with the notation "Gone. Left no forwarding address.")

One company-coming cooking endeavor was a success. The decision was made to feed the dinner guests roast beef. In 1948 I had an experience with beef roast cooking that turned out well. This background made me feel quite confident in suggesting I be the one to select the roast. The selection was a four-pounder with a rope around it.

Before placing in the crock pot I made six holes with the corkscrew. In each hole I placed a small piece of a garlic bulb. The final result was a tasty, tender piece of meat. (This corkscrew bit may be helpful to other novice cooks.)

The only thing that throws a shadow on that meal was failure to remove the rope before the roast went to the table. Cutting around it was no problem. I was careful. Other non-experts have since informed me the rope should have been removed in the kitchen. Trying to clear up this point for future use, all the cookbooks on hand were checked. The only information that might be relevant had to do with skewers holding things together. This cookbook was published in 1927 in England and says the skewers remain intact until you hit one carving at the table. Stick to the rope if you use an electric knife. You might get electrocuted.

A productivity analysis leads to the conclusion it may be better to go with the meat, bread and potatoes menu, when the results of kitchen activity have to be displayed. This has been confirmed by a non-cooking-until-retirement friend.

She said to me, "I've just worn myself to a nub trying to follow three recipes not even near each other in the cookbook. One of the disasters of this effort was a salad of cucumbers and onions cut up in lime jello. My brain didn't register the word 'congealed' until company rang the doorbell."

"Why didn't you remove the salad forks from the table and replace with spoons," was my helpful response.

After telling me to not interrupt, I learned the ultimate disaster for that meal was brought on by jalapeno peppers as she made an effort to duplicate a rice dish described on page 50 of her cookbook. When she mixed everything into the cooked rice, she used two peppers because they were so small. "Did you know jalapeno peppers are hot?" she inquired and then went on "Of course I didn't, but now I know. After getting everything mixed with the rice, I tasted. That mixture was so hot I singed my false eyelashes. And that's not all. While fiddling with the salad and the rice, the meatloaf burned, and I hadn't made the creme sauce to pour over it."

How people do this sort of thing day in, day out puzzled both of us. It's fun to do one special thing occasionally, but three? Or even four? At the same time? She didn't believe it could be done. We agreed. These cooks who make it to the table being hostess in a long dress must know something not included in our cookbooks. My friend said she took her guests out to dinner and came home worn to a frazzle to face a mess in the kitchen.

She has my sympathy. In case there are others who can't coordinate and don't savvy the lingo of cookbooks, I've written a few of my own recipes. They are designed to take the cookbook illiterate from the buying of the necessary, through preparation, cooking, and to the table sane. You'll notice none of the recipes pertain to cake. Too tricky by far.

## Crab Stew

Buy the crab meat. Leg meat is darker than body meat. A bit like chicken wings. A crab exercises his legs by swimming. A chicken flaps his to crow. Apparently this makes the meat dark. The white part of the chicken is called breast. The crab seems to have no breast. Just white body meat. Buy any kind of crab meat you can find, dead. Live crabs look sad when you kill them by dropping in a pot of boiling water. The water must be made tasty with things not appearing on your shelf, and if you do have them, you may not recognize them from the recipe. Too, you may have none of the tools necessary to get the meat out after you have extinguished life by boiling. Even if you have the tools, dead crabs are very stingy with their meat and free with their shell. You may end up with a handful of meat, half shell. The shell won't hurt the stew but it makes a crunchy sound at the table when you chew it.

So buy one pound of dead crab meat, any color, all ready to do something with. Select six potatoes, spuds not yams. Not too large and not too small. Peel potatoes. Be sure to cut out all the little eyes that have sprouted. They are listed by the Feds as being injurious to your health. (My grandmother said it better. They will kill you.) Split up and down. That gives you four pieces per spud. Cut again, roundwise, and drop in a pot (medium size) of water. Stand there and watch it until it boils. Steam will rise so don't put the lid on until you've cut the temperature in the eye. The water will push the lid up and it will run down the sides of the boiler into the interior part of the stove. Even if you have the eye holes covered with foil you still have a cleaning job or the expense of new liners. So don't let the pot boil over.

Cook the spuds until they are squashy. Set aside if you have a spot. If your work area is cluttered leave on the eye and cut it down as low as you can. But watch it. Lift the lid every now and then and smell to see if anything is sticking. Don't trust implicitly the readings on those knobs. If you burn the potatoes, you have to start over. Now get out a skillet. Turn the temp knob to medium. Put margarine in. If it is a stick, use about half of it. If it is in a tub, just estimate how much to make half a stick. Peel and cut up an onion. Any size. Put this in the skillet and push it around when the skillet is hot (but not too hot). Now add the onions to the potato pot wherever it is. Place in the same skillet you've been using about a half of a half stick of margarine you have left over. Heat. (There will be residue from the onion cooking.) Carefully put the crab meat in the medium hot buttered skillet watching for little pieces of shell (orange color) and white slivers similar to those found in turkey legs. (You can do this picking earlier if you have time, but you probably won't). After intense looking to pick, tumble around a few times. Add the crab meat to the spud and onion pot. Let that pot be until it's cool, then put in some milk. Pour and stir until you think it looks thick enough not to be soupy and thin enough to take a few saltines crumbled in at the table. If there is any sherry left in your bottle, add a dash at this point. If you are affluent and have cooking sherry, use that. (Set the pot back on the eye or turn the heat up, if you have not moved it. Season the stew. Salt and pepper and taste until you're pleased. The general rule of thumb is you can put it in but you can't take it out.) If your stew turns out to be soup which does happen sometimes, take corrective steps as follows: use the dirty skillet. Put half of a stick of margarine in it. Melt. Add a bit of flour and stir. Add a bit more and stir and stir, with vigor. When everything seems to be together, set it off. Add milk. Stir and stir. Add milk and repeat the stir until the lumps are gone. Cook again, briefly. Then scrape into the stew pot. Use a strainer if the lumps did not go away. A tossed salad is good with this stew. If you don't have the makings, dill pickles make a good vegetable substitute.

### Barbecue Steak

Buy about two pounds of that beaten steak, sometimes called minute. If you cook for solo eating, two small pieces will do, regardless of weight. Put about two big spoonfuls of bacon drippings in a small skillet. Turn the eye on high with skillet on it. When spitting, put the meat in, which you have cut in small pieces more or less one inch square. Sometimes they stick. Use a flat pancake flipper to turn, in a hurry. Set the eye control knob on medium. Put a lid on. Leave be for a few minutes. In this period mix the following in something: two or three big spoonfuls of brown sugar. (Careful here. The sugar crawls.) Shake the ketchup bottle with the top on. Remove the top and give a couple of good shakes over whatever you're mixing in. If you have bought barbecue sauce put in a couple of shakes. It's not thick like ketchup, so take it easy. Dash in a few drops of Tabasco and a little Worcestershire. Then a quick pass of salt and pepper. Mix all this with a big spoon. Use the same spoon and put the mix on the meat, which by this time has lost most of the juice you had in the skillet when you started. Cover. Wait. (About 10 minutes or until you finish doing something else. No hurry.) Find the tongs used to turn bacon and reverse each little piece of beef. At this point is a good time to put the rice on to cook. Just get your glasses and follow directions on the box. There usually is no trouble here. The only thing is reducing what the box says is two servings. They are trying to get you to eat a lot of rice and you may not want to. After everything is finished put the rice on each plate, and the meat and juice on top of it. If there are two plates to fix, count the pieces of meat and divide evenly. Kosher dills go good with this meal to give you a balanced diet. The drink can well be water because things are a bit hot.

### Brunswick Stew

Buy about four chicken legs, five if they are small. Don't get frozen ones if you plan to have the stew for supper, and it's already afternoon. At the same time you get the drum sticks, buy two or three thin pieces of pork steak. It looks like pork chops, but it's cheaper. While at the meat counter get about a handful of those stew beef chunks. You will also need a can of corn and a can of tomatoes. When you get home, wrap all the meat together in foil. Put it in a baking dish or on an old foil plate and cook in the oven until all is done. Let it cool. If you forgot to cut the fat off the raw beef and pork, do it now. Screw the food grinder to the table on the porch or wherever you do messy grinding. When the meat is cool, remove bones and cut up. Now run it through the grinder. I use a big dinner plate to catch the meat as it emerges. Next I run a good size skinned onion through. All that will go on one plate. Now I grind the tomatoes and catch in a bowl. If too juicy, drink some. If you use creamed corn you don't have to grind it. If you have the kind that isn't creamed, grind it. Now put it all in a pot. Add sugar, salt, pepper and Tabasco, a little water and some margarine. (Start easy, add more later). Heat, tasting often. This is where you add this and that. Then let it stew along for an hour or so, or longer. Or shorter. Stir often. Serve in bowls with plain white loaf bread on the table. Sweet pickles taste good with Brunswick Stew. So does iced tea with lemon.

## Salmon Salad

For two people buy a small can of red salmon. It will say *red* on the can, but it comes out *pink*. Don't cut the lid all the way off. Drain the juicy stuff into the sink. Now use your fingernail to lift the lid. Shake the salmon out into a pretty good size mixing bowl. Mash it up with a kitchen fork, not the good silver. Somewhere along the way you've boiled two eggs and peeled an apple. Get out the mayonnaise and sweet midgets. Skin a small onion.

Use the cutting board to chop the pickles, onion, eggs and apple (without the core). You can add celery, if you like it. I don't. Use a big spoon to put mayonnaise in the bowl with the mashed salmon. A dash of salt, pepper, Tabasco and Worcestershire go in with the salmon and mayonnaise. Mix. Add everything else. Now put in a little juice from the pickle jar and mix again. Taste and add whatever you think it needs. Serve on a lettuce leaf if you have it. If you don't, just put it on a naked plate. Nobody eats the leaf anyway. Iced tea with a dash of lemonade mix is good with salmon salad. So are crackers. If you don't have crackers, make toast in the oven with the knob on broil. Watch it constantly and turn. Then reverse and butter. Let the butter bubble, then turn off heat. Sometimes I dash garlic powder on the buttered side before bubbling.

## Hush Puppies

They are cornbread made to go with fried water food, like fish. If you are eating out, they are egg shaped or round and solid. I cook them flat because the big kind pose a biting into and handling problem. Sometimes you end up with a handful of corn meal crumbs. If you want 10 flat hush puppies for two people, two bite-size, use about a cup of meal. I like yellow but white will do. Just don't buy the pretreated stuff. It rises and puffs. Put grease in the skillet about a half-inch deep. Place on the eye on high and watch it as you get the meal in a bowl. Add one egg. Salt. Pepper. Garlic seasoning out of a shaker. One little onion really cut up. (Check the skillet. Cut the heat. Don't get the grease too hot.) Put everything in with the meal and egg. Add some water and mix. Keep mixing and adding water until you think it will slide out of a big spoon. Test the grease by putting a finger in the corn meal mixture and thumping finger toward the hot grease. You should get a little spit, not a lot. Now fill the spoon you mixed with and drop mixture, spoon by spoon, into the skillet. Don't let them nustle too close. They stick to each other. Stand by to turn. I use the pancake flipper. When brown (not dark) on both sides, take them up, and place on a paper towel and cover with same. Pat. You may have to add more grease to the skillet and more water to the meal, if you are cooking for four people. Anybody can eat five of these. If you've cooked 10 for two the original two may decide to eat six. So if you are cooking for four, better make twenty-four. If you are the hostess, go one short yourself until you see how things divide up.

## Goup

I have just finished making and serving goup for lunch. Acclaim from around the table was so favorable (two people), I think I have discovered a new treat. My problem is whether to share the secrets of this discovery with my public (two people), before I establish my rights. I'd hate for such a gastrinomical find to appear in print someplace without a credit line. Where to officially claim it is the center of my problem. I've written the Library of Congress for help. Do I need just a simple copyright? Or should I apply for patent rights? On the other hand, I may need a trademark with a slogan. Here are the steps in the kitchen and the ingredients needed to sort of duplicate my Goup. (Patent Applied For; Trademark Registered: Under consideration by Author.) Start with one pound of ground beef you want to last over six meals for two people. Half it. Place one raw half in a big pot. The other half goes in the skillet where you fried breakfast bacon and left the drippings. Work with the pot ingredients first. This is eventually going to be soup. Hold the meat pot under the tap and run in about two inches of water. Put it back on the stove on an eye turned to hot. Swish the meat around in the water. Cover. Watch and wait. When the meat has lost its pink, cut the heat half. Now start adding leftovers from the refrigerator. I usually can find half an onion (wrapped in foil in the vegetable compartment), some limp celery, a few butter beans, a bit of okra cooked with onions and tomatoes, the remains of an old head of cabbage and a few English peas. Things that need cutting up do so. Put all this in the pot. Add salt and pepper, slowly. Taste. If you didn't have any tomatoes with the okra, add one small can of tomato sauce. I don't make it too sharp with tomatoes. Indigestion. Now add things you didn't find among the leftovers. Like rice (a handful) and two small spuds cut up. Cover. Stir. Cook. Taste. After doing this for about 30 minutes, I usually have to add something. Maybe a bouillon cube. Now I can leave the soup on little heat (just an occasional stir) and go to the skillet to make the goulosh. Turn the eye up to hot. Scrape the other half of hamburger around in the bacon drippings to brown. Add big chopped up onion. Cut the heat about half while stirring the onion around with the hamburger until tan. Put in half a can of tomatoes. Disintegrate them with scissors if whole. Add half a can of creamed corn. Stir. Cover. Cook on low. After a bit add rice. Not too soon or you'll have to stir more. The amount of rice to add depends on existing juice. In the measuring cup I think the first rice addition would be about one-fourth. Add more later if you get too juicy. Now add salt, pepper and sugar. To taste. This is the most important part. Requires much concentrated thought with each taste. Goulosh needs to simmer along for a spell. The longer it cooks the better it is. But don't burn it. Add a bit of water if you've overplayed the rice. Next find a very big bowl. A mixing bowl will do. After the goulosh is done and the soup is through, mix them in the big bowl. Stir a good bit. Serve in bowls. The nice part about this recipe is you've got enough for six meals for two, maybe more. I think it has the minimum daily requirements of just about everything the body needs. And you only have two things to wash.

### Post Script No. 1

If you've invited a number of people to be your guests for a meal it may be wise to make it a potluck affair and let them bring the pot. The luck part is that things will average out, and you'll have meats, vegetables and salads contributed by your guests. The hostess furnishes bread, dessert and drink. Trying this recently for a jolly gathering, the law of averages split things fifty-fifty. Eighteen people came, and we had nine casseroles of macaroni and cheese and nine kinds of congealed salad. The decaffeinated coffee, part of my part, was good. The yeast rolls didn't come up very high but tasted all right. Since the guests took their empty dishes home with them, there was little washing up to dampen the spirit.

### Post Script No. 2

The best advice I can give to a budding cook is eat out. If you've been through Salad Daze, Salary Daze and are now in Retirement Daze and still don't know how, I think you would be giving Murphy's Law too big an edge. Everything that can go wrong certainly will. It costs too much to gamble. Look what happened to my cake. Even Murphy would have been overcome with the success of his prediction.

# AWAY FROM HOME

## AWAY FROM HOME

The meeting was devoted to a discussion of Objectives for Travel. The word vacation was not included because that is a permanent condition of the participants, they explained to me. Every day is a vacation for these 20 members of the Non-Pareil Club. They have a noon meeting twice each month in a private dining room at the local cafeteria. Their club slogan "From Rags to Social Security" is descriptive of the general atmosphere, when they gather for the pleasure of eating together, Dutch, and the discussion of interesting topics. The alphabetical roster of members, with husbands and wives listed in their own right, is used to determine who thinks up the next meeting conversation piece. The topic is revealed after the meal by the donor passing it out on slips of paper. No dues, no minutes, no officers. Note taking, if you feel the urge. I felt the urge, and here are the travel points made by the group: get there by public transportation, good food, reasonable prices, people, including children and things to see and do. I was silently thinking "no such place," when one man said he had recently had such a trip. As he detailed it: he had packed a bag, called a cab, traveled two miles to a downtown motel, registered, unpacked, put on vacation shirt and shorts, dark glasses and with a paperback, settled in by the pool. He informed us he enjoyed watching the kids in the pool and talking with parents from different states. He found agreement among travelers on avoiding the interstates, but no agreement on what other routes were best. Some had better rest rooms. Others had better restaurants. He now knows the price of gas in seven states and that all vehicles get good mileage on regular. He said he tanned in three days, read four books and all the newspapers, ate good food, called a cab and went home. Total cost $84.60 including very small tips. Interesting conversation with the travelers was possible because he left his wife at home. She immediately informed us she was going to do the same thing next month, leaving him at home.

 If I want to let my travels take me further from home than advised by the club group, I scan a map of the U.S. It hangs over my desk and is dotted with colored pins. They indicate the locations of friends or kin. A red pin means don't go back soon. A blue indicates use but not overuse. A green says try it. Enough greens scattered around can provide maybe supper, bed and breakfast for a nice trip. It is better not to phone or write. Just drop in late in the afternoon. After chatting, inquire about motels in the area.

 My greens worked just fine on a recent trip to the mountains. This was a legitimate green pin invitation to spend the weekend. When up that way I also enjoy checking in with other acquaintances who have for years earned a good, dishonest living with a copper coil back in the hills. This time I got quite a shock. They have gone legal and are selling gasohol wide open down on the highway. I received assurance the Snake Pit Still was intact, and they could easily switch products if the need arose.

We enjoyed recalling past excitement the winter four of us, females, answered a midnight call for help. We were playing bridge, but we sallied forth in a drizzling, cold rain to help push a pickup truck load of sugar out of the mud. The truck was stuck on Snake Pit Trail, and word had come, via lightning, that the law was roving. We pushed the truck into the bushes and got down the trail with 30 minutes to spare before the revenuers struck the Pit. They got nothing but wet.

This trip in 1980 found the same non-athletic females, over 30-plus-plus, still keeping fit by reading about new diets, lugging boxes up a hill to pick butter beans. The roadside sign read, "Butter beans 10¢ a lb. You pick." In thirty minutes we reassembled at the roadside stand to have our pick weighed in. Each of us had about 25 pounds. We were traveling in a four-door gas saver. Since we were on the way home, the trunk was filled with four overnight cases and eight totes. The owner of the car left three of us to guard the butter beans and departed to find an auto supply establishment. She returned with a luggage rack on top. After buying and filling leaf bags with the pick, we managed to slowly cover the 200 miles home with four big bags giving a whistling concert from topside.

I'm not going to dwell on shelling those pretty beans. My advice is think three times before tackling something that sounds easy, and you have had no opportunity to practice in quantity. I'm settling for a piece of tissue paper on a comb. If I can make music, I'll join colleagues of my age who are known far and wide as the Comb in Three Parts Band and have no inclination to freeze vegetables.

One travel venture by plane turned out all right but not without incident. The incident was snow. There were 64 of us weather stranded in a motel at the airport. We lounged around looking grim and worried about those connections being missed. Not a jolly group. But that changed at meal No. 2. One brave soul stopped undercover maneuvering to take his pills and boldly lined three bottles among the sugar, salt and pepper. The "Oh, you take high blood pressure medication. So do I. Mine look like this" started. That unfroze the climate inside. It didn't take long for one gentleman to collect a dime from each of us to make a most-different-pills pot. Would you believe one of the weather hostages was taking seven different kinds of medication? And that didn't count aspirin, but did count non-prescription tablets for when her stomach buzzled. Since this was a cross-section of the general population selected as at random as you can get, one may safely say the average U.S. citizen takes three pills per meal for buzzling stomach, high blood pressure and no energy. This is why we build our defense forces around automated military hardware. Most of us don't have the strength to squeeze a trigger.

 The urge to get on with visiting the wider world was sparked by the 1980 sailing schedule of the QE2. With the help of a magnifying glass I went through my possessions looking for the magic word: "Sterling." With a paper bag full of silver goodies I visited one of the "we buy gold and silver" places. This negotiation made possible a visit to the travel agent where newly acquired funds were exchanged for a round trip reservation to Southampton, England on the Queen, stateroom 5083 located in the basement. Finding an agile companion to use the upper bunk was no problem.

 That is how August 1980 found me again waving to the Statue of Liberty. I was a paying passenger on Queen

Elizabeth 2 and I was on my way back to England.

I had last waved to the Old Girl holding that torch in the harbor in November 1945. As the tug boats brought the ship in, 14,000 of us waved and cheered from the decks of the Queen Mary as a dock-side band played *Sidewalks of New York*. We cried and we cheered. For some it had been several years since leaving that port in the dead of night and zigzagging across the Atlantic dodging German subs.

Travelers on the younger Queen have delightful choices available to fill the five-day trip. The difficulty is deciding whether to become more proficient in body skills, be made more attractive in beauty scope, improve the golf swing, learn ways to save tax dollars, challenge the brain on current events or find a soft deck chair in the sun.

One day I attended the lecture on legal tax shelters. All one has to do is buy oil drilling equipment, store it somewhere like in the yard and let it depreciate. The depreciation is deductible. I tried to keep up with the arithmetic the lecturer was giving us on a chalk board but the amount of money needed for that deduction ran off the edges of the board and my brain. However, I'm glad to know about these things. I have a better understanding of things on view in yards here and there. Little rusty deductions.

One noted newspaper columnist took a whack at the big publishing companies. In his morning lecture he accused them of stifling writing talent with sensationalism. Unless you are a public servant crook just out of jail or famous for some other caper, your non-ghosted manuscript won't ever get a reading. His thesis supported the publishers who gamble with the author sharing the cost of the chancy business of being published. If you can't figure out a way to go to jail without staying too long and have had to buy another stick file for rejection slips, do it yourself.

The further down you go toward the bottom of the ship, the less you pay for your cabin. If you have double-decker bunks and no porthole, you pay even less. Those of us traveling Transatlantic could easily watch for whales from dozens of glassed-in-decks, free. Not only that, but when the Queen had a bit of rough seas to ride, portholes contributed nothing to helping passengers retain things. When I was topside and wanted to go down to the cabin, there was no trouble finding an elevator and remembering to punch the last button in the sequence.

There were many interesting things to research. Having tea on the balcony which also contained shops, I had an excellent view of a gentleman trying on a white dinner jacket in the Men's Shop. His wife was assisting him. She thought the split tails pulled open too much across his rear. He didn't buy the coat. This was my first opportunity to observe the male in such a shopping habitat. He seems to get more assistance from the female than vice versa.

So far as was observable under the influence of *Dramamine*, there is a very thin line between the haves and have nots. There was no distinction in the lounges. The bartender took everybody's money. There may have been more Bloody Marys on the tables of Senior Citizens who looked like they had been demoted to Chairman of the Board. Martinis were more often held by people young enough to be on the way up and not so far up they left the olives.

Clocks were set forward an hour each night. If one retired at 1:00 a.m. it was 2:00 a.m. This played havoc with the feeding on demand system. By the time the hungry cycle made the adjustment, we were in Southampton, arriving at the hotel at 7:30 p.m. just in time to eat again.

No problems checking in. The only small hitch occurred when we found our room cluttered with male clothing. That was resolved quickly by the maid who called the desk and said, "You boo-booed." They moved him out, whoever he was. We dressed in our flimsies and went down to eat a hearty five-course dinner. The restaurant was crowded. We ordered and began. The fire alarm sounded in the middle of the fish and everyone in the hotel was evacuated. After 30 minutes of standing outside watching the fire trucks in a cold drizzle in our dinner attire with no wraps, the all-clear message came. When we returned to the restaurant, the waiter offered to warm the fish, but somehow warmed-over broiled fish made us even colder. We settled for a tart from the dessert truck and coffee.

It was 11:30 p.m. the same night. I had finished my preparations for bed and was in it. Everything was in place on the bedside table: tissue, nose drops, flashlight, travel clock, a few caramels, aspirin, reading glasses and a paperback. I had smashed the pillows, and they were just right. Nothing unusual except the location of the room. It was on the seventh floor. The fire alarm sounded again. In preparation for the trip abroad the needed things were packed first and then the in-case-of-need batch. I forgot to include two sheets. When the alarm sounded, I mentally related the on-hand blankets and sheets to the distance to the ground. If I went that way, I would be hanging four floors high. In making a decision of that nature it is best to follow the crowd. I evacuated down the stairs in a short rain jacket with the hood in place, looking neither to the right nor left. At least my cover had a zipper and I didn't have to clutch the closure.

It all turned out all right. False alarm. But I've been pondering the decision-making process set in motion by events which could have finished me off. Probably it is better to accept the age-old wisdom, "You can't take it with you." A few valuable minutes were lost trying to answer the question "If you can take some of it with you, what do you take?" I took the caramels and the unfinished paperback and left my money under the mattress. It might be said my concerns lie along a hunger-leisure-time dimension even if headed for heaven.

We used the time next day between morning breakfast at 8:00, 11:00 tea, lunch 1:30, tea at 4:00 and dinner at 8:00 to plan our itinerary for the eight days before the return of the Queen from the Canary Islands. Everything worked out. We managed to depart Southampton each day either by train, bus or hovercraft. Our line of travel extended from Southampton to Brighton and Cardiff with London and the Isle of Wight thrown in as dividends.

Nothing marred our jaunts. Not even being offered Senior Citizen discounts at a few ticket windows, including Cardiff Castle, whose history dates back 1900 years. In touring the Castle we were warned there were 87 spiral steps to the top Tower Garden, and we might wait and rejoin the group after the up and then down part of the tour. I met the most forward of the group on their way down, but I made it to the top. It wasn't even a good garden. Just dahlias, like those on the ground. I rested among them for a few minutes until my calves unknotted and stopped quivering. No trouble going down, except I had to remove my glasses.

We had spent two months packing and unpacking for the trip to England. The weather reports all summer indicated very cold weather in that country. Packing warm clothing at home in a temperature hovering around 100 degrees isn't easy. You just can't believe you'll need flannel pajamas, wool suits, fur-lined coats and fleeced boots. But believe it, we did. And spent the day at Brighton on the beach in our wool suits with everyone else in bikinis.

We went by train to renew our memories of London. One exciting, very vivid and pleasant memory of 1945 has to do with a call from the U.S. Embassy telling us Her Majesty, the Queen (now the Queen Mother) had expressed the desire to visit our unit May 14. Would we care to extend an official invitation? Our reply, "Delighted," set things in motion and the invitation was officially extended. This led to a call from Buckingham Palace. The Chief Inspector in charge of security for the Royal family desired an appointment to come around and check floorboards and things. He checked every inch of the planned itinerary.

No hitches anywhere. Her Majesty arrived on time, in her 1930 vintage Rolls, accompanied by Lady Hamilton. The greeting, "Welcome, Your Majesty," came as we shook hands. Her response, "It is a pleasure to be here and to thank you and your troops in person for your efforts on behalf of my country."

A one-hour visit had been planned. The one hour extended to three and passed all too quickly for us of the United Kingdom Base unit, 37 Upper Grosvenor Street, London, England. We loved her.

This year, 1980, I was there as she celebrated her eightieth birthday. I wish I could have chatted with her about old times. She would have appreciated my recalling having sung *There Will Always Be An England* in a pasture in Cheltenham just after D-Day in 1944. The U.S. troops were celebrating the Fourth of July. Our hastily assembled four piece band could not play *The Star Spangled Banner*.

The British Rail System remains the same. You can get anywhere by train. All you have to know to board the right one to transport you is the number of the track and the departure time. Find that track and get aboard whatever is standing three minutes before time to depart. If the miles to be covered in the trip number forty, the train will stop about forty times. You get off at the stop time quoted for your destination. The schedule is precise to the second.

Inside, the train is designed for passengers to sit facing each other. Or a traveling animal. My eye-to-eye companion on one trip was an English bulldog. He was on "hold," his owner explained to me. No leash.

Everyone smokes. In spite of the big ads in all stations warning Her Majesty's subjects the Surgeon General of the United States has determined smoking is dangerous to your health.

Speed is of the essence in England. Our cousins are a bunch of shifting people. The streets, highways and byways are jammed with small vehicles propelled by very expensive gasoline and four-on-the-floor. It behooves the driver to take it through the gears to high as quickly as possible. When traffic moves from a halt it takes off in one fast leap. If you are a pedestrian you stay put on caution, or you'll be pancaked by the first gear shift taking her to twenty.

Food is more costly than petrol. Keeping within a very limited eating budget was made possible by careful selection of places to eat. We gave Italian, Indian, Chinese or Col. Sanders eating establishments our business for a big meal each noon.

We literally flew to the Isle of Wight by hovercraft. That vehicle skims along the top of the water at breakneck speed. When the port is reached wheels appear, something like a collar deflates, and you are driven up a ramp to the station. From there you walk. One mile uphill buses are loading for a tour of the island.

If you can make it up, do so. We did and had a delightful day seeing history and reading road signs. One sign we saw many times: "Ice, Sweets and Chance Machines." They don't call them slot machines. Whatever they are called, you can drop your shillings in a hurry.

Traffic directional signs along the way were unique but clear. I especially liked 'Look Left' at one crossroad. The driver had been warned 'Slowly Now' before he was told from which direction to expect trouble.

After nine delightful days in England, we boarded the Queen for the five-day return trip to the U.S., broke and hungry. The hunger part was more than corrected by three meals and two teas every day at sea. Deficit financing continues.

The deinflated U.S. dollar was worth more on board ship in the Sportsman Club than anywhere else we went. The One Armed Bandits sometimes gave cherries, three for one. That represents a nice profit. Unless you decided to try for oranges, ten for one. Or none.

In Penn Station in New York it took $5 to do a $1 job of moving suitcases from the sidewalk to the AMTRAK luggage room. Even with three $1 bills prominently displayed there were no Red Caps. The fiver brought three. That is inflation.

I have made no judgment on whether it is better to take little trips or blow it all on one big one. If the IRS doesn't audit me over that expense deduction for the trip to England, I just may try China next year.

If you've caught up with fun traveling and had enough retirement time around the house and really itch to get back to work and have no visible saleable skills, join the antique trotters. These are antique dealers who usually have no shops. They keep the stock in boxes whose contents are placed on display in a ten by twelve foot booth which is rented from a promoter. This rental is done in advance. To get to wherever the show is being held you do your trotting in a truck, van, auto, camper or hitch and pull. You don't have to be an antique yourself, but it helps. The public seems to have more confidence in grey-haired dealers, even if it is dyed some other color. They can tell.

I can give no advice on how to acquire your stock, but it must go into whatever vehicle you plan to use for travel. If most of the things you want to sell are your own and you have enough to fill four ten-foot tables, covered with cloth, you are lucky. In getting price tags on, multiply by fifty whatever you think it originally sold for. You can always have a sale, if you've gone too high.

You will need shelves on the tables. When everything is flat, it isn't very attractive. Three or four or more boards placed on painted two-pound coffee cans provide nice uplifting.

If you have to buy your stock, stay home. Just taking x-number of dollars for change and expenses often stretches the sock money. You can't count on liquidity from the show. It may be one of those times when all the other ninety-nine dealers do well, and you don't sell a dime's worth.

If you get it all together and on the road, don't forget to take a dark blue or black outfit to wear everyday. And do take a dog. You will probably get a drafty booth, being a new dealer. A shaggy dog to keep under the table on your feet is a real comfort. A word of caution. Check with the vet to see if your dog's tranquilizers are different from yours. Dogs sometimes must be quieted. I saw a show disrupted by a female poodle being the center of attention for all the male canines owned by other dealers. The owner of the poodle had to wrap her in a lace table cloth ($100) to get her out to the van. The dealer and the poodle shared tranquilizers.

There are things you will do well to know about operating your business. An expertise in making change, wrapping a package and keeping an eye on the stock at the same time is very helpful. Sometimes you get home and find you are missing some item you haven't sold. You also have to have an iron constitution to keep that 'I'm not watching you' face, when someone ignores your PLEASE DO NOT HANDLE sign, picks up one of the six cut glass tumblers signed, *Tuthill*, and thumps it.

Speaking of cut glass, *Russian cut* refers to glass, not a grain embargo, and *Brilliant Period* when used in the antique trade, also refers to cut glass, not the Jeffersonian political era.

Other antique vocabulary may mislead you. *Quilted satin* does not refer to bed cover. *Dame Nancy* is also tricky. If the cameo vase is signed like that, it was probably not made in France, but by some nanny in England. It is also very helpful to know a bit of written Chinese. Paper labels on the bottom of their thought-to-be early enamel-on-copper vases may read "Made in China for Imperialist Americans." If you don't know any Chinese, remove all labels.

Have a reply ready for the inevitable questioner who wants to know how you know it is an old piece of whatever it is. Don't say your great, great somebody brought it over on the Mayflower. They are overloaded now.

It is very good to have something unusual enough to attract the crowd. A good example, George Washington's wooden teeth.

Stay out of jewelry except for your own use in ears, etc. Knowing all the precious, semi-precious and unprecious stones would stump Socrates. Selling isn't so bad, but buying is a hazard.

Selling silver appears to be easy. It isn't, unless you

know all about Troy, not Helen, weights. You'd be surprised how little silver is in some silver, but gold is even more tricky. The weight has to be reduced like calorie cutting, and you could get in a mess as you ascend and descend with weight and gold content. You also need a hot line to Wall Street, London, Zurich and Japan to see how things are going that day. It's okay to sell at yesterday's quote, if today's report is lower. It's the reverse that puts you out of business.

The best advice I can pass on is have a quick cash sideline, such as selling shoe polish and doing demonstrations. Don't do silver, every dealer polishes that.

If you don't own a dog or if for some other reason you can't join in the business of selling antiques, you might go the route of collecting. This gives you a good, legitimate reason to spend money for gasoline to drive to the antique shows to spend money for your collection. Usually someone can be found who is free to join you for the little trip and help cut cost. Hopefully you'll get home with a tank full of whatever propels your car.

Use care in selecting the category and the specific item you would like to own. You don't want to find one of the things too often. That could deplete your collecting fund in a hurry. Cut glass is nice to collect if you are looking for something along the line of a left-handed buggy whip with a cut glass handle. There will usually be several displays of cut glass and the dealers will take your name and address, just in case they run across the whip you want.

Silver is also good to collect. Just go far enough back in time to pinpoint your wants. This may require a bit of research on your part. Something similar to a goblet used by Robin Hood could set the search in motion. If some dealer finds it and writes you a complete description, including the word sterling, you would be wise to check it out.

I have a friend who started collecting thimbles. She now has a good big collection and is currently looking for the gold thimble used by Betsy Ross when making the flag. That is known as specializing and becomes necessary sooner or later, depending on your money. I think it is easier to start that way and open the gate an inch at a time.

When the very thing you have adopted for your special hunt begins to turn up in quantity, you may safely assume someone is currently turning them out. This business of reproducing is big business and keeps people employed. Unless you want to get in on that angle, perhaps you would be wise to change your wants. Too many left-handed buggy whips with cut glass handles can ruin the market!

# REAPING THE HARVEST

## REAPING THE HARVEST

Just mention a box lunch to me and I can activate memories grounded in my first teaching experience, when lunch was included in the $20 monthly for room and board. The only thing in plentiful supply in the early '30s on that farm was sweet potatoes. I took baked potatoes out of the lunch box every day — no matter what else was included. "You have to have a filler," said our landlady. Running the yams a close second was the non-cooked sliced apples and mustard between two pieces of homemade loaf bread sandwich. Boiled eggs got in the box every now and then, when the hens cooperated. It was necessary to extend the noon recess period to allow time for the lunch to decide which way it was going. To have clanged the bell too early would have been a mistake involving teachers and pupils, since everyone took the same type lunch. This was before the day of the non-filling balanced diet lunches provided by the schools.

I did go on a picnic not long ago. My contribution was

in a fried chicken box with a well-known name inscribed thereon. Practically everybody brought the same thing. Those who didn't came in with kidney bean salad, but even at that it was a picnic, and it was fun. The ants were given a chance, but without sweet potatoes and apple sandwiches they may soon become an extinct species. I couldn't help noticing ants don't look as robust as they did when fed a filling noon meal of sweet potato skins.

School lunch boxes aren't alone in long ago experiences from which I am currently reaping dividends. Learning acquired in grabbing clothes on very cold 6:00 a.m. mornings and running to the one fire in the "sitting room" to dress has been reactivated. Perhaps the running has slowed a bit, but the fireplace has returned to the center of activity. Of recent date I've even remembered to cover the remains of the fire with ashes at night and to put a piece of "lightard" on the hearth, ready for morning blowing.

Even current baseball game watching on TV is reaping a harvest. At best baseball is slow. I have time to wonder where the ball goes, when some slugger bangs it out of the park. Long ago experience taught me to run inside the school house, when a muscled player connected his bat with the ball. We had no fence. Our joining land at that country school was a cornfield. The owner waited for the ball to encroach on his corn. Then he hid the ball and came over to read us the law about trespassing.

In the TV games I watch today, nobody seems to worry about where the ball goes, when it goes. But I do. I think about the cost of a baseball. A good one could be bought for 30 cents in 1933, if you could travel the ten miles into town to buy it. We had a baseball rule: you knock the ball in that cornpatch, you walk to town and buy a new one. We became very short on long hitters, unless we had a visiting team. Then a small lad hid in the corn and retrieved the ball. The visiting team brought their own ball, bat, gloves (if any), and catcher's protective front garment. Our catcher couldn't remove his to lend. We laced him into a corset quilted in front by the sewing class. It laced in the back; so he had to wear it all the way through the game. It didn't look like a corset because of the dark brown color. The cooking class dipped it several times in a big boiler of strong tea. The catcher had to be warned about sliding in, when he got a hit. There was the possibility he might dislocate a stay and be stabbed. He was advised to be called out safely.

One of the most amazing things currently taking some of my leisure time is the weather report. Imagine knowing it's going to rain in the p.m. without moving outside to take a look. I once thought I was a better than average rain predictor. Every morning at 9:00 a.m. the sky had to be surveyed, a prognosis made, and the two school bus drivers told what time to return. The roads were not paved. The red clay turned to mud when it rained. In order to get the children home before dark, school "let out" at 1:00 instead of 3:00, if water was descending from heaven. Not many wrong calls. No one objected anyway. Including me.

If your past experiences give you a chuckle, by all means recall them. They are good to lean on, and often help us understand some of the things we do and don't do as wise seniors. Don't buy a new preowned car without having someone poke a finger in the differential oil hole. My first auto was a used A-model Ford with sawdust in that grease place. I've had a good many cars since then. All okay. But I still want the sawdust possiblity looked into.

Sometimes we regret having spent our money-making years making no money. I've just seen a listing of top golf, tennis and bowling professionals with their take for the past three months. Staggering. I obliterate regrets by rationalizing they, too, move on into senior brackets as their muscles dry up. Toward the end it all evens up for Social Security.

In going through boxes of stuff you've accumulated, check for written material. In addition to pressed flowers and old prom cards you may find a poem or two composed in your youth. I've found several poetic literary efforts tucked away with a third place ribbon won in a posture contest. I'm trying to decide whether or not to expose the poems to public view. Here is a sampling:

### AT THE THEATRE

"I'm so sorry," she mumbled,
As across my feet she stumbled.
Very quietly, there she sat,
Resting comfortably on my hat.

Not bad, is it? Then how about this one:

### FEET

On to work they spryly go
Without directions so and so
In spite of corns and knotty lumps
I'd rather have feet than knee length stumps!

Time marches on, and I'm pleased to be with it. In cadence, or not.

As far as music is concerned, I've never been in step. Having one musical ancestor in the family tree hopes were high that mother and father had passed the musical genes to me. The first effort to uncover the talent was made through violin lessons. Something was lacking. I was in my first recital at the age of eight. My father fainted. After that he was protected from having to listen to my performances which went on until I broke an arm. There were those who called this accident a blessing.

Even if I never learned to play with gusto, the rewards have been great. When someone is playing the violin, anywhere, I listen and enjoy it. I can close my eyes and locate that beautiful sound scrambled into a symphony. My admiration for the violin players knows no bounds. And sympathy. Just thinking about all those after school and Saturday lessons it took to get them into that concert makes me want to give them a pat on the back to go with the applause.

My artistic ability did have a brief opportunity to blossom. The watercolor class was doing still life composed of apples, oranges and grapes stacked on a piece of green velvet with fringe. One by one the bunch of grapes turned into a stem. I shared the guilt with the other class members. From then on we painted empty vases. None of my work ever got posted.

But the gain was there. I know what a flat painting is, and that it isn't desirable. I had that word inscribed in red pencil on all my efforts, and today I can spot it a mile away.

I've been unable to trace my late blooming writing talent. If anything is illustrated, it is you don't know whether you can or cannot write until you try. I had one teacher in grade seven who made us diagram sentences all year. I never connected that with writing or anything else. Neither did I see any point in learning to use a dictionary, until I discovered all those forbidden words contained in it. Now, in trying to get my thoughts on paper, I actually can skip the bad words as I check the dictionary to see whether to use further or farther. I'd say if you can spell well enough to be able to locate words in the dictionary and can tell a verb from a noun, you're in.

First you write, and then you scratch it out. Even if all goes into the trash basket, it helps time to pass — and who knows? You may find you have a bud on those roses you've expected to find.

Sometimes we reap something we have not sown. But more than likely there is evidence in the past to support the person we have become. They do tell us we are what we have eaten. I like to expand that with when, where and with whom. Even if we've consumed milk and other things from bottle to bottle, people, time and places have been involved. There is always a setting. The nice thing about all this is today finds a base on yesterday, and tomorrow is reaping time from today's doings, retired or not.

# SAVE FACE

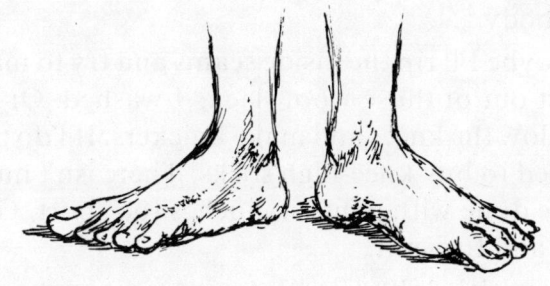

## SAVE FACE

After a few months of retirement the gloomy feeling of being put out to pasture will go away. No longer will that lost feeling creep in at moments like when you go to bed. Bedtime thoughts begin to slide into little grooves of pleasant anticipation of the challenge for tomorrow. Last night my in-bed thoughts went like this:

1. I'll stop and look at the T-bones when I go to get the hamburger.
2. What can I do with four green tomatoes? Three weeks is long enough to wait for them to tinge on the vines.
3. There must be something to stop that hose leak. Changing my clothes every time I turn it on and again when I turn it off is just too much.
4. How much cash will I need to save money on all those off coupons in the kitchen drawer?

5. I'll try lighter fluid on my toenails. I don't believe there was a warning label not to wear dyed shoes in the rain. I'll check that. Could be I can sue somebody.

6. Maybe I'll rip the inside seams and try to make a skirt out of those wool slacks I washed. Or cut off below the knees and make knickers. If I do that I'll need to buy knee-high socks. There isn't much can be done with pants six inches too short. Give away and forget it.

7. Wow! It's 1:30. Glad I don't have to get up at 6:00 a.m.

8. I think I'll try to cut my hair in the back. Or maybe I'll call for an appointment and have it cut. It looks so taggy, I'm ashamed to go to the beauty parlor. I'll see what I can do first.

9. Must not forget to soak those two stamps off. After all, forty cents is 40 percent. Can't beat that even with money markets.

10. What makes the living room curtain fall every time the front door is opened?

11. Check the gingerale and ice cream before tomorrow night. Or maybe serve that fruit that's been fermenting so long. I might win a rubber if I get my guests whoopy.

12. These glasses are no good for bed use. They stop up my nose.

13. Where did I see that recipe for cooking an elephant?

There is no feeling in all the world like awakening in the a.m. with an elephant on your mind or a good, strong sense of purpose. If by chance you've awakened too early, turn over and resume sleep. This may take practice. Pretend it's 1:00 a.m. and go through the old relaxing routine. You are an old stocking with no garters or whatever to hold you up. Sleep creeps in as the stocking goes down. When you are awakened by nature, about two hours later, get up, go to the bathroom, look in the mirror and take a cold shower. After several mornings of this routine you may want to stop looking in the mirror, if you are still unable to accept what you see. Don't stop. You'll eventually get to know all the cracks and crevices, and begin to fight back with every grease being bottled for the expressed purpose of filling the cracks. Try them all. You may find one that does. The most time consuming activity of a retirement day is getting ready to meet the unretired population looking like one of them. Even if you have no other objective than to find that elephant recipe.

So far as I know, the educated retiree has no advantage over the less educated in adjusting to retirement. I've had no opportunity to obtain data to speak to the hypothesis "less education, less retirement difficulty at age 65." Being a nation of educated people or people in the process of being educated, probably there would be no one to study at the education deprived end of the scale. We are all very much alike, anyway. Nursery school, kindergarten, elementary school, high school and college. Not quite the cradle to the grave, but almost. It figures out at about 20,000 hours or more to bring us to our present condition.

Parents who get their children through the education hours of life do occasionally get confused. My neighbors educated one of their boys to be a doctor and the other to be a lawyer. They are in a constant domestic uproar at their house. Every little accident warrants a sue or cure decision.

Even with the fads, frills and weak spots, schools take us up the ladder to adult independence and the good life. I have a feeling these two things do not peak out, when the word retirement rears its head. Possibly the top rung of that education ladder is always just out of our reach, and the fun of retirement is to keep feeling for it and try to enhance things. That may be all there is to the good life at any age. Keeping the brain lively and the body elastic. And you don't necessarily have to do either. Especially if both are stiff.

That's why I'm in a quandary trying to find the answer to the question: "Does a Little Old Lady look better in dresses or pants?" Just when one becomes a Little Old Lady is not clear. By age I may be, but by temperament I'm not sure. Replacing front zippers with the billowy waist gathered to a skirt seems to tip the balance in favor of age. I begin to look and feel like those pictures of females who need estrogen-androgen. Or the projection of another miracle in multiplication.

The foundation garment people are not much help in scrambling signals. Restraining and reshaping the female figure from the neck to the knees is their business. They understandably are not concerned about the barrel effect their undergarments give the figure, since short necks and thin legs don't come into the underwear category. Even the effects of a face-lift to help the neck is of no help if negated by parts unlifted. So I vote for pants for those of us in the cover-up group by age or heredity. This includes men. After looking at my male friends I've discovered quite a few LOM. Their problems seem to be a shifting of the center of gravity as appendages get thinner and the middle gets thicker. Most of them look better in long pants than short pants. Deliberately attracting attention to the upper end is part of their strategy, too. Perky caps with emblems go with the costume. The beltline is concealed by a flowery sport shirt. Improvising body cover-up may be the closest bond between men and women as time bumps into our ego props.

Another segment of my retirement act involves hair. It gets worked on at odd times not related to anything else. Cutting my own hair was the logical place to start doing likewise to my stardard of living. In its natural state it was thick, grey and straight. Do-it-myself expertise has changed it to thick and thin, orangish and frizzy. It requires little or no coiffure effort on my part. Nothing can help it. Next time around I'll use the pinking shears more systematically, give myself a permanent, and then use the color-toner.

This sequence comes on page 3 of the little home permanent booklet, and I failed to see it the last time until the "gently unwind" stage was upon me. Thoughts about using a wig were discarded. My hair is thick. The wig slowly rises.

One sop to shrivelling old age is to take inventory of your attributes. Mine have never been staggering at any age. They still aren't. Two left feet remain constant. I could at one time give myself a plus from the ankles to the knees. The plus has been deleted. It would have been nice to have been two inches taller to have allowed for present shrinkage. The ascent to the age of wisdom has left some small traces of what I started with. That's ego. Damage to the original is due to lack of exercise. I'm trying at this late date to correct some of that.

I started last week with kicking in the pool, hanging on the side. On the way from the pool to the ladies locker room music floated. Being of a curious nature I opened the gym door to see if the Charleston had been replaced by the waltz. It had. Thirty or so college age males were "point front" and "back," "point side" and "back," "point side" and "step" to the Blue Danube or something. I joined them. It was some minutes before the football coach spotted me and slowly pointed his way to my back row. The dancing teacher kept things going for about ten minutes before a break.

The coach then informed me ballet was the best practice his team could have. It made them light and quick on the hoof and kept them from looking like muscle clods. He said he was glad to have me and invited me to come again. I didn't go again. Not because there is danger I might get to look muscle cloddish, but by the time I could put my heels on the floor football season was over.

I keep up the kicking in the pool but repeated darning has made my suit heavy in the seat. I may have to give bikinis another try, if I can't replace my short-legged wool leotards. Bathing suits with little skirts and top cups are not for me. The skirts billow in the water and the cups live up to their name, fully. It's tricky to leave the pool with everything down and in. Having only two hands means crawling out in a crouched, clutched position until everything is checked.

Exercise doesn't seem to help other ego areas of decreasing competency. My memory for example. In the big city recently I couldn't remember where I was staying. Brain wave gaps. I'd just bought a comforter on sale and asked the clerk to have it delivered to the hotel. When I couldn't close the gaps to produce the hotel name, I said, "Oh, I'll just take it with me. I'm due back for lunch anyway." The salesperson put the comforter in a leaf bag. No tote hold. Getting from fifth floor bedding to ground floor exit with my arms around a double bed comforter couldn't be done on the escalator. My feet were hidden. Finally the elevator was located, and I made my way bumping person-to-person to the street. The leaf bag made a good seat at the curb so I could signal a cab. Then

I remembered. I didn't know where I was going. When a cab finally stopped, I stuffed the package in first, fell in on top of it and panted, "The nearest hotel." Would you believe it? That was it. I recognized the look the doorman gave me as I tried to get through the revolving door with my leaf bag.

I had thought my little lapse of memory would take the prize. Not so. One of my street neighbors wins hands down. Her husband was out of town for several days attending a meeting of the Silver-Haired Legislature to which he had been duly elected. She took advantage of his absence to do a bit of yard work. Being very fatigued that evening, she had a bite of supper and went to sleep during the evening news. The ringing phone awakened her. Their son, who is employed several states away, wanted to talk to his dad. She said, "Wait a minute. I'll call him." Thereupon she searched the house and yard calling loudly. She was almost in a panic before she remembered her son's father had been gone three days. She has not revealed how she explained that loss of memory to the holding-on-the-line son.

Being interviewed on TV once, about a bit of writing I had produced and managed to get before the public, I went absolutely blank. The interviewer said he had read a review of my brainchild and credited it with having both wit and wisdom and he wanted me to give the TV audience an example of the wisdom in the book. I couldn't even remember the title. My answer was: "When ignorance is bliss 'tis folly to be wise. The readers' judgment is far better than mine in interpreting my writing gems." Then I went home and read the book.

My decision making process seems to have slipped a bit, but I'm working on that. I've always admired people who give clear-cut, quick answers to questions like "Are you free to go to the play Tuesday night?" I've started quibbling with that "if" answer. Usually iffy people really mean "yes," if nothing better turns up. My trouble is thinking I might want to do nothing, but I'm doing my best not to hold things up on the horns of an "if."

Save face. When you get through doing all the things you need to do to make yourself presentable, go anywhere with the results —except back to your old work hole. You just ask the ego to stand that kind of exposure, and you'll have a headache for a week. It is also very hard on employees who are still there. They put on false smiles, when you appear in the office door or someplace, all the time thinking about that report due two hours from now and wondering where they could take you for deposit with another colleague. You don't continue to be "good old Joe who once worked here" very long. They gave you a good-bye rocking chair in hopes you would mount it and be gone. We tell ourselves it isn't that they don't like us. They really don't want us snooping around seeing how things have gone to pot without us. If things look better than ever, then where are you? A "don't call on them, let them call on you" philosophy could save all faces.

I've discovered another face-saving technique from a farmer friend. He was making a most unusual row pattern as he ploughed a field with a nice new tractor. His rows looked like they might have been made by someone who had sampled fermented apple juice. I found there was a simple reason for the zig-zag pattern. He shifted tractor direction with the wind. His explanation, "If I addle sideways, I can spit easy. No back-put. If I spit straight into it, tobacco juice covers my glasses. If you can't, don't. Lots better than having to clean my glasses every time I spit."

# NO DOUBT ABOUT IT

## NO DOUBT ABOUT IT

The on-sale item you go back to buy has been sold.

When the gas guage shows empty, it is.

If the invitation reads "casual dress," you'll be the only one casually dressed.

Bathing withers the skin.

Christmas cards come from the people you forgot to remember.

Teeth won't get any whiter no matter what kind of toothpaste you use.

Those brownie spots are not freckles.

Nothing will hide those brownie spots.

If you couldn't at age 20, you still can't.

Your pulse is skipping when you count it.

It isn't the temperature when you're too hot or too cold.

New magazines will continue to show models who are tall, thin and necky.

You need a larger pill box.

Trip mileage is figured in terms of your back.

You say you don't like food you can't chew.

All interesting people are your age.

Your gore churns when you get a notice from a broker recommending "safe" investments.

You invest safely.

There are no turkeys at a turkey shoot.

When a baseball flies into the stand, it is not returned.

When a tennis ball flies into the stand, it is returned.

A lad sitting on top of a big gas station's outdoor sign is waiting to change the price upward.

When something looks havey-cavey, it is.

The paper boy will continue to throw the paper on the roof.

Pig slats are not spareribs.

You look better in a small mirror.

The name you can't remember when confronted by the owner is Smith.

When you try that bikini at some place far from home, someone will yell your name.

You will avoid easy chairs without arms.

You balk at giving up your big gas guzzler.

You think little autos are not safe.

You have trouble going from successful living to living without success.

You don't need a tax shelter.

You need an IRS shelter.

The sermon lasted 20 minutes, not 40.

Speakers mumble.

You turn off the commercial showing a young thing snickering at an older female who is hard-of-hearing and has bad breath.

You usually know what year it is.

You will often have to inquire as to what day it is.

You never know what time it is.

Neither bifocals, trifocals nor no focals make it possible for you to see your face in the bathroom mirror.

Splitting nails keep splitting.

You feel uneasy in tennis shoes.

Things won't get better.

Things get worse.

If things are as bad as they can be, you're in trouble.

Some young brain will publish another pit to avoid in making a will.

Your new will is in the pit.

Nothing helps indifferent gray hair.

The brain is more active than the body.

Women are women.

Men are men.

The twain continue to stalk a meeting.

Faulty memory excuses untruth.

Many things begin to fall into the "let somebody else do it" category.

Feel great and would like to do things; nobody calls.

Have a cold and feel terrible; three opportunities ring the phone.

The figure with the sweater reading, "Your Pad or Mine?" is not looking at you.

If these things go too far, you are too far gone.

A mortuary near the hospital gives an uneasy feeling.

You wish for the good old days when you had a family mechanic, plumber and physician.

If at first you don't succeed, you won't.

To shrink needs, stretch dollars and inflate ego is asking too much.

Retirement represents the fulfilling no wants span of time.

If you do rubbings from old tombstones, you will need knee pads.

Communicating through overt expressive behavior a well-balanced sense of self-worth is done by the employed.

Finding necessary expedients to cope with expressive behavior indicating a well-balanced sense of self-worth displayed by the employed makes the retiree sick.

The Happy Hooker establishment sells fishing equipment.

The "5:00 p.m. to 7:00 p.m. Attitude Change Period" sign over the bar door does not refer to personnel counseling.

"If you see one, there is always another" refers to snakes and patrol cars.

Time is of the essence, but without money there is no essence.

Army Generals and Navy Admirals don't become Senior Citizens.

There is no such thing as a left-handed stamp roll.

A penny saved is never worth as much as a penny earned.

If there is a way in, there may not be a way out.

It gets harder to label things "junk" when trying to throw away.

Sit through one TV program after another and get a flattened outlook.

There is no point in avoiding activity that has no point.

Pre-retirement thoughts about going from rags to Social Security have changed to alteration possibilities.

July and August bellies are in pens, not at the beach.

All we want is a chance to make the same mistakes.

If you've been retired one-hundred twenty days, the honeymoon is over.

Your vocabulary is significantly larger at age sixty-five than it was at forty.

You will continue to add to your store of words.

It takes you longer to find stored words.

You should try to think of the things you don't have and don't want.

Making nothing successful stumps the young person.

Older people are good at making nothing successful.

To confront age you make adroit use of all assets.

You don't have enough assets to confront age.

You will expand your assets as you confront age.

The unclipped thorns make it hard to find the rose buds.

You will continue to say, "I retired early."

## THE END

(However, there's more! Turn the page.)

## PERSONALLY

I was born near Grant Park Zoo in Atlanta. Maude, the elephant, was my first friend. That accounts for my enduring interest in elephants. Early childhood activities probably are at the root of my "keep busy" feeling. My first job assignment, age 3, was to keep the swirls in the legs of the sewing machine dusted.

Academically I was neither slow nor fast. I got an "A" once in the 4th grade for a map I traced at the window. College days are shadowed by being campused for various activities such as leading a barnyard melee that made the dorm ceiling fall.

And so it goes. At present I'm trying to stack up enough things today to give direction to tomorrow. As one bricklayer, age 85, said to me recently, "It ain't how you laid 'um once, it's how good you lay 'um today and tomorrow."

Georgia B. Watson

In addition to the author's comments about her achievements, *Who's Who* tells us she has a string of academic degrees including the Doctor of Philosophy from Peabody College of Vanderbilt University and a year as a Post Doctoral Research Fellow in Psychology at Yale University. She now holds two emeritus titles: Professor of Psychology and Head, Psychology Department, School of Arts and Sciences, Georgia Southern College, Statesboro, Georgia. When asked about these things her reply, "Yes, and the hardest part of starting a new career is to keep from leaning too hard backwards."

The Publisher

## WHY DID I DO IT?

I've been asked why I wrote this book. Leisure time bores me flat. That's why. Just so much of it is enough. I begin to feel like a lump of dough without the stuff in it to make it rise. My decision to look for little rays of sunshine for those of us who seem to be surrounded only by signs of growing ancient has made me feel better. Motives are never evident. We infer their presence only after an action. The book reveals the stirred up state of this organism that produced it. Isn't that something! I did it. There isn't any message in it. What prodded me to take my pencil in hand was probably a guilty feeling. Hearing a lot about retirees having earned their leisure made me realize I'd never worked hard enough to deserve as much as I was getting.

*Georgia B. Watson*

Additional copies of "Life in the Retirement Bed of Roses" may be ordered by sending $6.50 plus $1.50 postage and handling for each copy desired to:

    Rainbow Books
    P.O. Box 1069
    Moore Haven FL 33471